11 plus

Maths Practice book
With
Topic wise exercises-
Age
10 to 11 years
Book 1

11 Plus Math's Practice Book with Topic-Wise Exercises Age 10 to 11 years Book 1
ISBN 9781326990916

Table of Contents

CHAPTER 1 - FRACTIONS

A Fraction is a part of a whole. Fractions show parts of a whole number for example, the fraction $\frac{1}{5}$ shows that are 1 part out of 5.

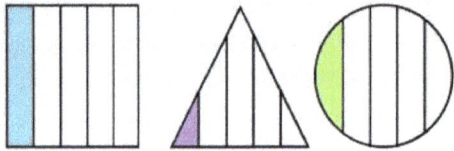

Half the fraction is shaded.

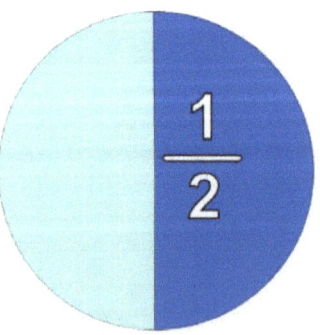

Fractions
Exercise 1.1 (Basic level)

Tell what fraction of each shape is shaded.

a)

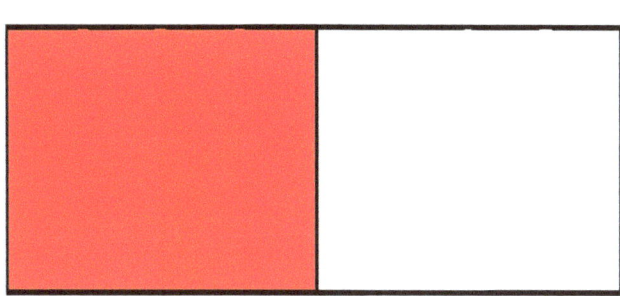

Answer ⬜

b)

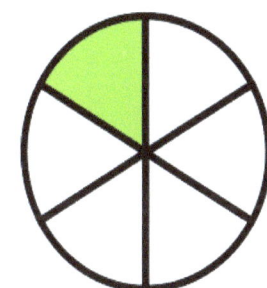

Answer ⬜

c)

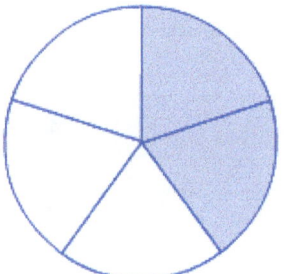

Answer

d)

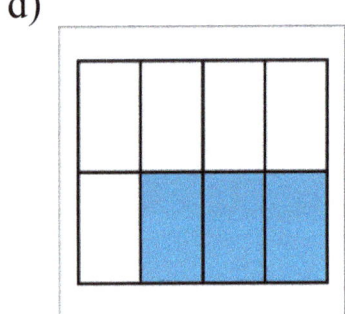

Answer

e)

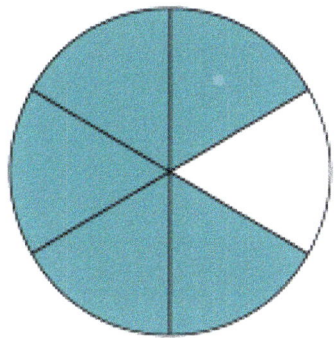

Answer

f) Tell about blue -shaded one

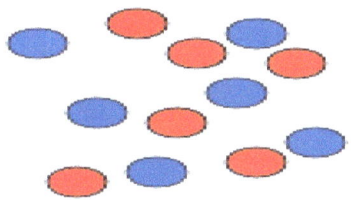

Answer

SCORE

2. Advanced Level (Adding and subtracting fractions)

a) Adding or subtracting the fractions with the same denominators=
it is easy to add and subtract fractions when the number on the bottom
is the same . These are called denominators.
For example, =

$$\frac{2}{5} + \frac{6}{5} = \frac{8}{5}$$

b) Adding or subtracting fractions with different detonators
Sometimes the fractions don't have the same denominators.
In that case, we find the highest common factor for the denominator.

For example, =

$$\frac{1}{2} + \frac{1}{3} =$$

A common multiple of 2 and 3 is 6
Now you can add them together.

$$\frac{1}{2} \times \frac{3}{3} = \frac{3}{6} \qquad \frac{1}{3} \times \frac{2}{2} = \frac{2}{6}$$

$$\frac{3}{6} + \frac{2}{6} = \frac{5}{6}$$

$$\text{Answer} = \frac{5}{6}$$

c) Equivalent fractions = Two or more fractions are equivalent if they equal the same value irrespective of their numerators and denominator.

For example, $= \frac{2}{3} \times 2 = \frac{4}{6} \times 2 = \frac{8}{12}$

d) Multiplying and dividing fractions

Multiplying fractions is easy. You multiply the top numbers,
Multiply the top numbers and multiply the bottom numbers.

For example, =

$$\frac{3}{5} \times \frac{2}{6} = \frac{6}{30}$$

For dividing fractions, keep the first fraction is

changing the divide sign to multiply and flip the second

fraction upside down.

For example, $= \frac{3}{5} \div \frac{6}{10}$

First step change sign ÷ to ×

$$\frac{3}{5} \times$$

Second step flip the second fraction

$$\frac{3}{5} \times \frac{10}{6}$$

Third step simplify the fraction if needed.

$$\frac{3}{5} \times \frac{10}{6} = \frac{30}{30} = 1$$

3. Advance (Mixed Fractions and decimals)

A mixed fraction is defined as a fraction formed by combining a

whole number and a fraction. For example, if 8 is a whole number and 12 is a fraction, then 812 is a mixed fraction.

Example: Convert $3\frac{1}{4}$ into an improper fraction.

To convert any mixed fraction to an improper fraction:

Step 1 – Multiply the whole number by the detonator.

Step 2 – Add on the numerator

$3 = 3 \times \frac{1}{4} = \frac{12}{4}$ and now add the numerator

$$\frac{12}{4} + 1 = \frac{13}{4}$$

Example: Convert $\frac{7}{5}$ into a mixed number.

$7 \div 5 = 1$ whole one and 2 remaining.

We write it as $\frac{7}{5}$ or 1

Exercise 1.2 (Advance) – Fractions

Follow the instructions and find the answers for the following fractions.

1) Add the fractions.

$$\frac{1}{4} \;+\; \frac{2}{5}$$

a) $\frac{3}{9}$

b) $\frac{13}{20}$

c) $\frac{3}{20}$

d) $\frac{9}{20}$

Answer

2) $\quad \frac{2}{3} \;-\; \frac{4}{9}$

a) $\frac{2}{6}$

b) $\frac{2}{9}$

c) $\frac{4}{9}$

d) $\frac{11}{9}$

Answer

3) Is. $\frac{1}{8}$ less than, greater than, equal to $\frac{1}{2}$?

a) less than ½

b) greater than ½

c) equal to ½

Answer

4) Reduce the fractions $\frac{27}{36}$

a) $\frac{27}{36}$

b) $\frac{9}{12}$

c) $\frac{7}{9}$

d) $\frac{3}{4}$

Answer

5) The shaded shapes below represent fractions. Which fraction is the correct solution to the problems?

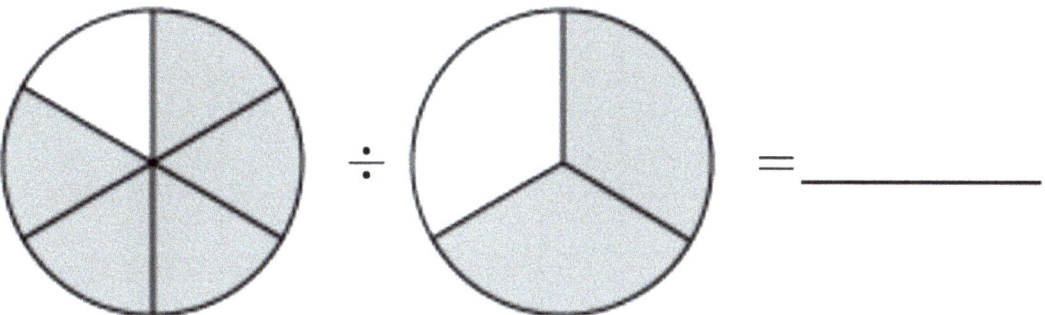

a) $\frac{5}{4}$

b) $\frac{4}{5}$

c) $\frac{5}{9}$

d) $\frac{9}{5}$

Answer

6)   Solve this equation:

$5 \div. \frac{1}{4}$

a) 5

b) 20

c) ¼

d) 1

Answer

7) $\frac{3}{7}$ of grade 8 play football. If $\frac{3}{5}$ of the grade 8 are boys, what is the fractions of the 8th grade boys play football?

a) $\frac{6}{12}$

b) $\frac{36}{35}$

c) $\frac{9}{35}$

d) $\frac{3}{5}$

Answer

8) $\frac{3}{15} \div . \frac{1}{5}$

a) $\frac{3}{75}$

b) $\frac{3}{5}$

c) $\frac{1}{3}$

d) 1

e) 5

Answer

9) Ajay spends 1/3 of his money. He then spends 1/3 of what he has left.

What fractions of the money did he spend altogether?

a) $\frac{5}{9}$

b) $\frac{2}{9}$

c) $\frac{1}{3}$

Answer:

d) 4

10) Divide fraction $\frac{1}{15} \div \frac{1}{30}$

Answer:

11) What is 1/3 of 414?

a) 124

b) 102

c) 138

d) 100

Answer:

1 2) $\frac{2}{3} \times 72$

a) 12

b) 48

c) 24

d) 36

Answer:

13) Find the difference

$3\frac{1}{4}$ - $2\frac{3}{4}$

a) $1\frac{2}{4}$

b) $\frac{3}{4}$

c) 1

d) $\frac{2}{4}$

Answer:

14) Convert $3\frac{2}{10}$ to an improver fraction.

a) ½

b) $\frac{19}{5}$

c) $\frac{31}{10}$

d) $\frac{32}{10}$

Answer:

15) Raj rode his bike $1\frac{3}{4}$ miles to a friend's house and then $3\frac{1}{4}$ more miles to the library. What is the total distance, in miles, that Raj rode his bake?

a) 4

b) 5

c) $4\frac{1}{2}$

d) $5\frac{1}{2}$

Answer:

16) Andrea is $5\frac{1}{2}$ feet tall, Sita is $\frac{2}{3}$ foot taller than Andrea. How tall is Sita?

a) $5\frac{1}{3}$ feet

b) $5\frac{3}{5}$ feet

c) $6\frac{1}{6}$ feet

Answer:

d) 6 feet

17) Multiplying the number by 2 by which of the following with the result in a product greater than 2?

a) $\frac{3}{4}$

b) $\frac{1}{2}$

c) $\frac{4}{3}$

Answer:

18)　solve $15\frac{5}{8}$ - $3\frac{1}{3}$

a) $12\frac{1}{2}$

b) $12\frac{1}{24}$

c) $10\frac{7}{24}$

d) $12\frac{1}{3}$

Answer:

19) Sue had $2\frac{5}{6}$ pizzas left from her party. What is that amount rounded to the nearest whole number?

a) $2\frac{1}{2}$

b) 3

c) 4

d) 5

Answer =

20) Sam is following a recipe for pizza sauce that calls for ½ teaspoons of parsley.
He is using a measuring spoon that holds 1/8 teaspoon.
How many times will he need to fill the measuring spoon
with parsley to make the pizza recipe?

a)5

b) 10

c)15

d)8

e)12

Answer

SCORE

Exercise 1.3

Complete the equivalent fractions.

1. $\dfrac{}{3} = \dfrac{12}{18}$

2. $\dfrac{9}{12} = \dfrac{81}{}$

3. $\dfrac{18}{} = \dfrac{90}{125}$

4. $\dfrac{3}{} = \dfrac{18}{24}$

5. $\dfrac{}{2} = \dfrac{7}{14}$

6. $\dfrac{}{6} = \dfrac{36}{54}$

7. $\dfrac{2}{} = \dfrac{8}{36}$

8. $\dfrac{}{5} = \dfrac{6}{15}$

9. $\dfrac{}{7} = \dfrac{2}{14}$

10. $\dfrac{}{2} = \dfrac{4}{8}$

11. $\dfrac{3}{4} = \dfrac{30}{}$

12. $\dfrac{6}{12} = \dfrac{}{72}$

13. $\dfrac{}{10} = \dfrac{8}{80}$

14. $\dfrac{1}{} = \dfrac{5}{15}$

15. $\dfrac{2}{6} = \dfrac{12}{}$

16. $\dfrac{}{8} = \dfrac{42}{48}$

17. $\dfrac{3}{5} = \dfrac{24}{}$

18. $\dfrac{}{25} = \dfrac{24}{50}$

SCORE

Exercise 1.4

Multiply fractions

> I can multiply fraction

1. $4 \times \frac{1}{2} =$ _____

2. $7 \times \frac{1}{4} =$ _____

3. $5 \times \frac{9}{10} =$ _____

4. $\frac{2}{3}$ of $2 =$ _____

5. $\frac{5}{8}$ of $1 =$ _____

6. $\frac{1}{2}$ of $1 =$ _____

7. $\frac{1}{6}$ of $3 =$ _____

8. $10 \times \frac{4}{5} =$ _____

9. $\frac{1}{12}$ of $5 =$ _____

10. $6 \times \frac{6}{12} =$ _____

11. $\frac{4}{8}$ of $3 =$ _____

12. $3 \times \frac{1}{10} =$ _____

13. $\frac{2}{4}$ of $2 =$ _____

14. $\frac{1}{2}$ of $4 =$ _____

15. $9 \times \frac{4}{6} =$ _____

16. $3 \times \frac{1}{3} =$ _____

Chapter 2

Ratio

Ratio in maths, is a term that is used to compare two or more numbers it is used to indicate how big or small quantity is compared to the other

For example:

There are 3 blue shaded and 1 not shaded squares.
you can write them as
3:1

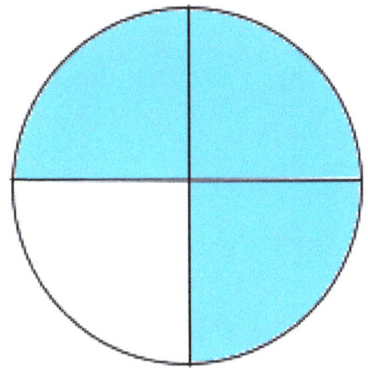

Example: - Simplifying ratio

12:20

The ratio can be simplifying same as fractions

$\frac{12}{20} \div 2 = \frac{6}{10}$ You can simplify it further $\frac{6}{10} \div 2 = \frac{3}{5}$ as ratio it can be written as

3:5

A proportion is an equation in which two ratios are set equal to each other.

For example – if there is 1 boy and 3 girls you could write the ratio as

- 1:3 (for every 2 boys there are 3 girls)

- 1/5 are boys and 3/5 are girls

- 0.25 are boys

- 25% are boys

Exercise 2 (BASIC RATIOS)

I can simplify Ratios

1. 12: 16 [ ]   2. 5:20 [ ]   3. 2:6 [ ]

4. 21:15 [ ]   5. 20:90 [ ]   6. 15:25 [ ]

7. 72:90 [ ]   8. 42:54 [ ]   9. 88: 99 [ ]

10. 54: 48: 36 [ ]

11. 45: 120: 135 [ ]

12. 26:52: 104 [ ]

13. 56: 63: 77 [ ]

14. 36: 60: 72

15. 13: 52: 117

16. 60: 90: 150

17. 9: 18: 27

18. 60: 108: 98

19. 360: 630: 7680

20. 63: 84: 126

Score

Exercise 2.1 (Advance Ratio)

1. Chocolates are on sale 6 for £10. How many chocolates can you buy for £15?

a. 8

b. 9

c. 10

d. 11

Answer

2. Ram can read 45 pages in 30 minutes. What is his reading rate in pages per minute?

a. 135

b. 15

c. 1.5

d. 2

Answer [   ]

3. Minnie has 4 pairs of low top sneakers, 7 pair of high-top sneakers, 3 pair of sandals, and 1 pair of boots.
What is the ratio of the pairs of low-top sneakers to the total number of shoes?

a. 4 to 15

b. 7 to 15

c. 4 to 3

d. 1 to 2

Answer [   ]

4. There are 176 slices of bread in 8 shelves. If there are the same number of slices in each shelf, how many slices of bread are in 5 shelves.

a. 110

b. 173

c. 100

d. 163

Answer [   ]

5. Sophie saved £39. the ratio of Sophie's saving to his brother Jackson was 9:4. How does Jackson save?

Show your working out

Jackson =

6. Aryan and Alex were given a total of £240. They shared the money in the ratio 5: 7. Work out how much money Alex received.

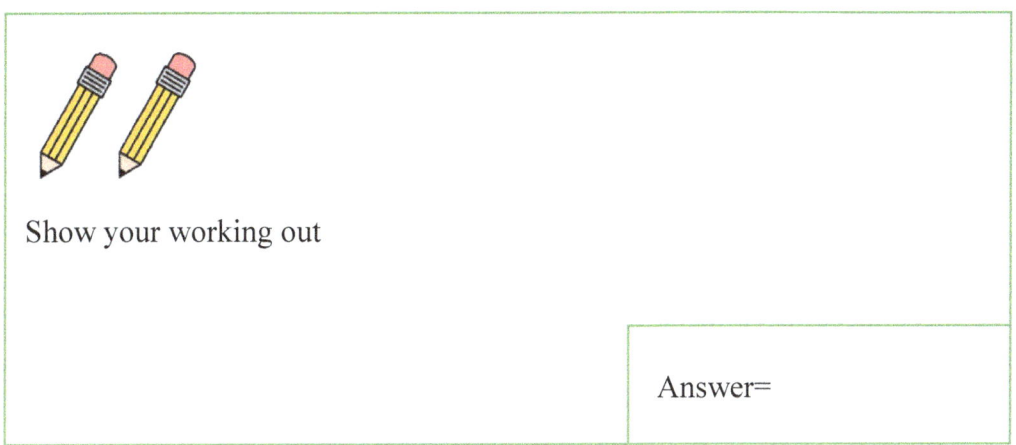

Show your working out

Answer=

7. At Alexander shop, a multipack of 8 toilet rolls costs £2.40.

At Alexander shop, the cost per toilet roll is twice as much.

How much is a pack of 3 toilet rolls at Alexander shop.

Show your working out

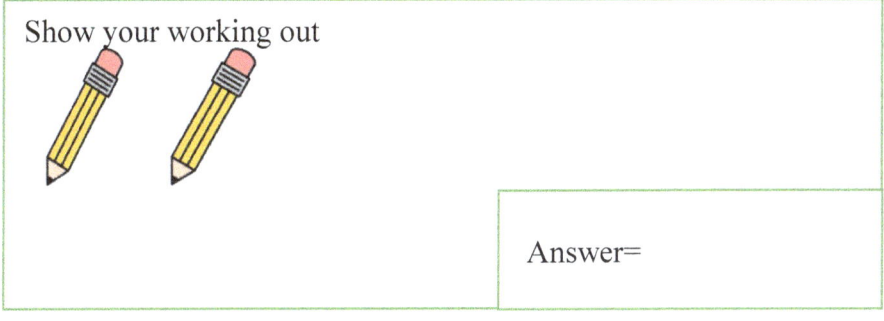

Answer=

8. Peter and Sam share £80 in the ratio 3:2

Work out how much each of them get.

Show your working out

Peter=

Sam =

9. Milly, Zoie and Ella share 42 sweets in the ratio 3:2:1
Work out the number of sweets that each of them receives.

Show your working out

Milly=
Zoie=
Ella =

10. 54 children get on a coach 23 of them are girls. How many boys ?

Show your working out

Boys

11. An estate is shared between Julie, Jack, and Jill in
the ratio 2: 3: 5. If Julie received £2400.
How much did the others get?

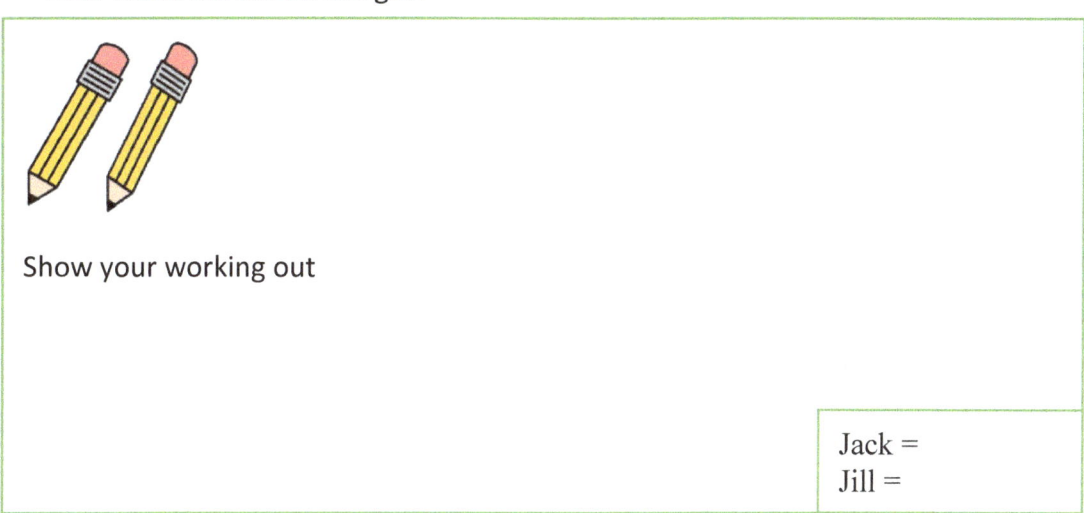

Show your working out

Jack =
Jill =

12. 3 people win £120 in the lottery. They spilt in the ratio 1: 3: 8. How much does
each person get?

Show your working out

Answer=

13.Jenny and Neil share some money in the ratio 2:3
Neil gets £900
Work out how much money Jenny gets.

Show your working out

Jenny =

14. A jar contains 600 beans. Of all the beans. 2/3 are red beans and the rest are orange beans . What is the ratio of red beans to
Orange beans?

Show your working out

Red beans=

Orange beans =

15. In Rebecca class there are 12 girls and 20 boys.
What is the ratio number of
a) Girls to boys?
(b) Boys to total number of students?

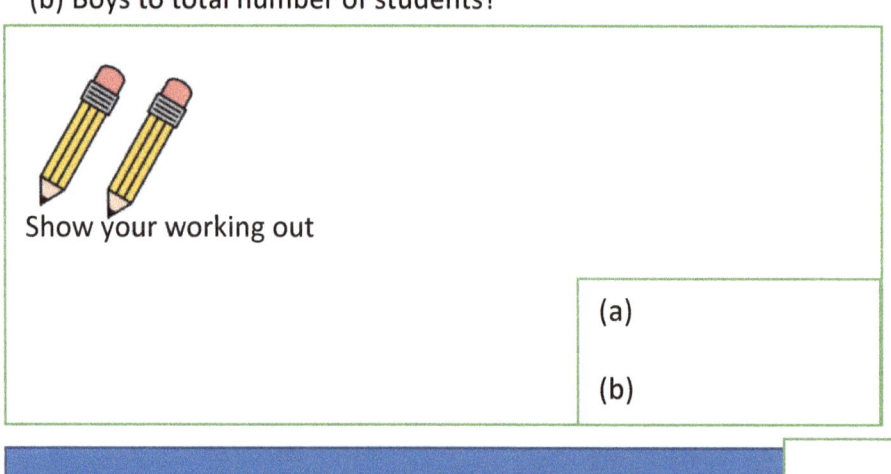

Show your working out

(a)

(b)

SCORE

Exercise 2.2

Doubling and halving

1. Double of 36

Answer:

2. Half of 84

Answer:

3. Double of 94

Answer:

4. Half of 108

Answer:

5. Double of 198

Answer:

6. Double of 8

Answer:

7. Half of 98

Answer:

8. Half of 82

Answer:

9. Double of 190

Answer:

10. Half of 18

Answer:

11. Double of 65

Answer:

12. Double of 178

Answer:

13. Half of 1874

Answer:

14. Double of 190

Answer:

15. Half of 168

Answer:

Score

Chapter 3
Percentage and decimals

Percentage is calculating by dividing the value by the total value, and then multiplying the results by 100. The formula used to calculate percentage is Value /total value x100%

Example:
10% of 20

$\frac{10}{100}$ x 20 = 2 Answer

To change percentage to a decimal, divide by 100.
For Example: Change 50% to a decimal.
50÷100 = 0.48

A percentage can be expressed as a Decimal or a fraction.

For Example:

Half can be written as

50 in percentage
0.5 as a decimal

Exercise 3 (Basic)

Convert Fractions, Decimals and Percentage

	Fractions	Decimal	Percentage
1.		0.23	
2.			84%
3.	49/100		49%
4	75/100		
5.	98/100		
6			17%
7	92/100		
8			80%
9	27/100		
10			44%
11		0.12	
12	35/100		
13			56%
14	99/100		

Score

Exercise 3.1 (Advance)

1. A factory produces 1,250 model cars. The quality control person finds 8 cars that are defective. What percentage of cars are defective?

Show your working out

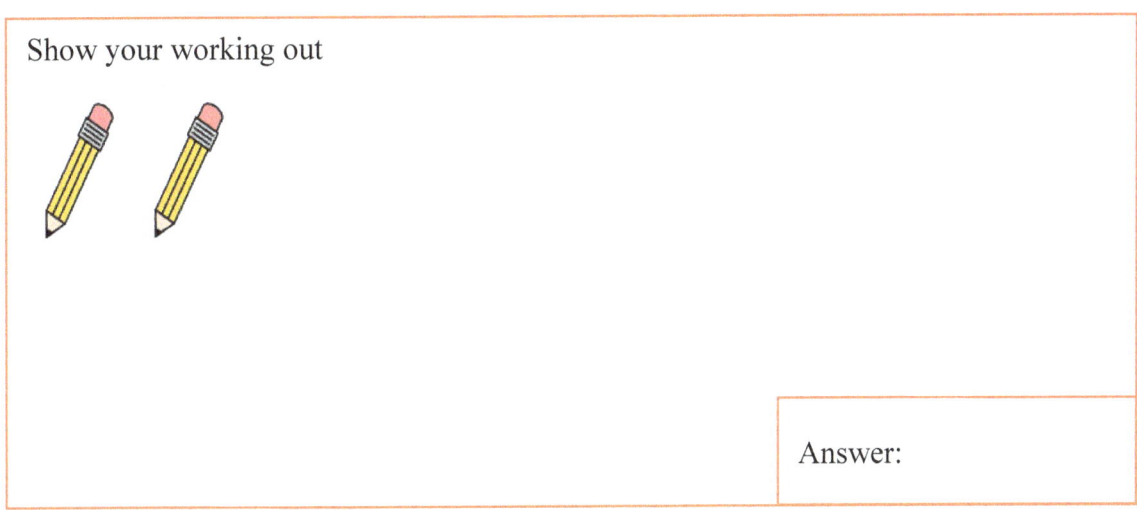

Answer:

2. Reena got a 74% on her Social Studies Test. The Test had 50 Questions. How many questions did she not answer correctly?

Show your working out

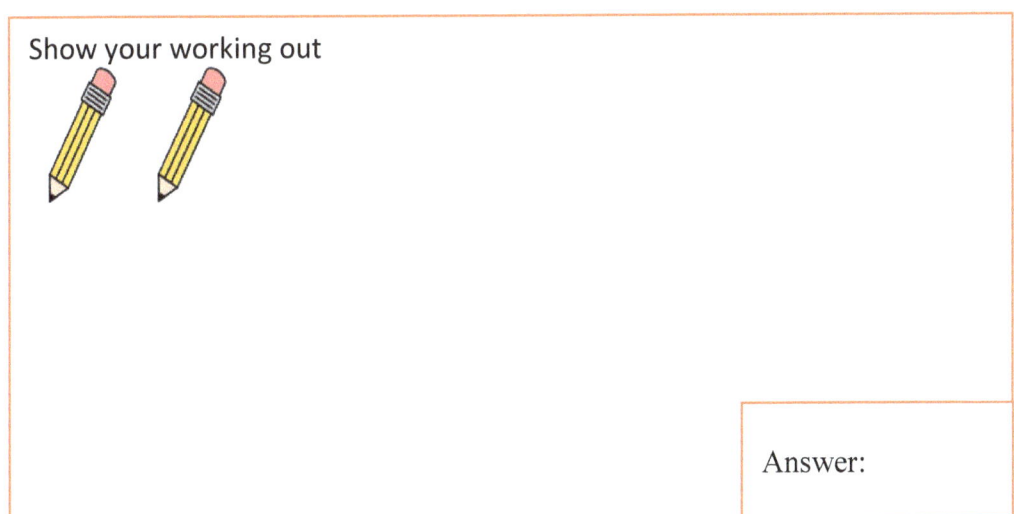

Answer:

3. Mr Wilson purchases a 5 – pound bag of apples. If apples cost £1.50 before the 30% discount, how much does Mr Wilson pay for a 5pound bag?

Show your working out

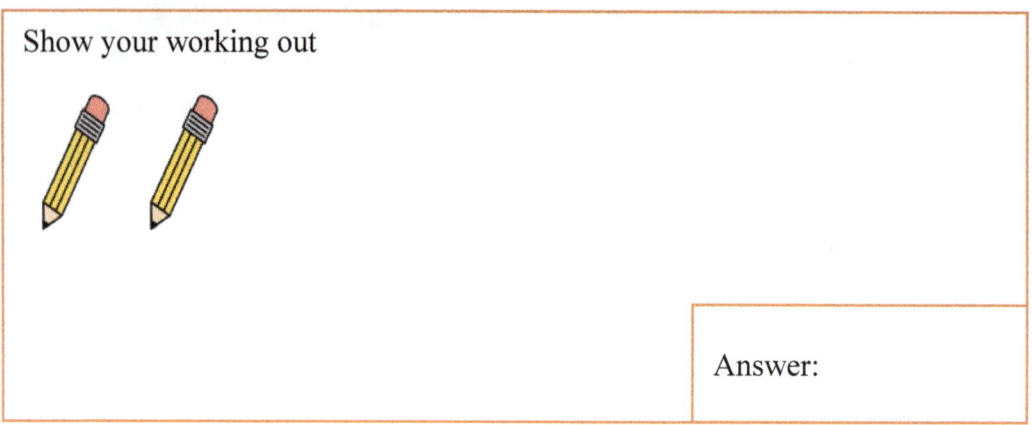

Answer:

4.

Given the information below:

Of the boys surveyed - 5 preferred volleyball, 30 preferred basketball, and 15 preferred softballs.

Of the girls surveyed - 30 preferred volleyball, 5 preferred basketball, and 15 preferred softball.

Out of the 100 students surveyed, what percent preferred volleyball?

Show your working out

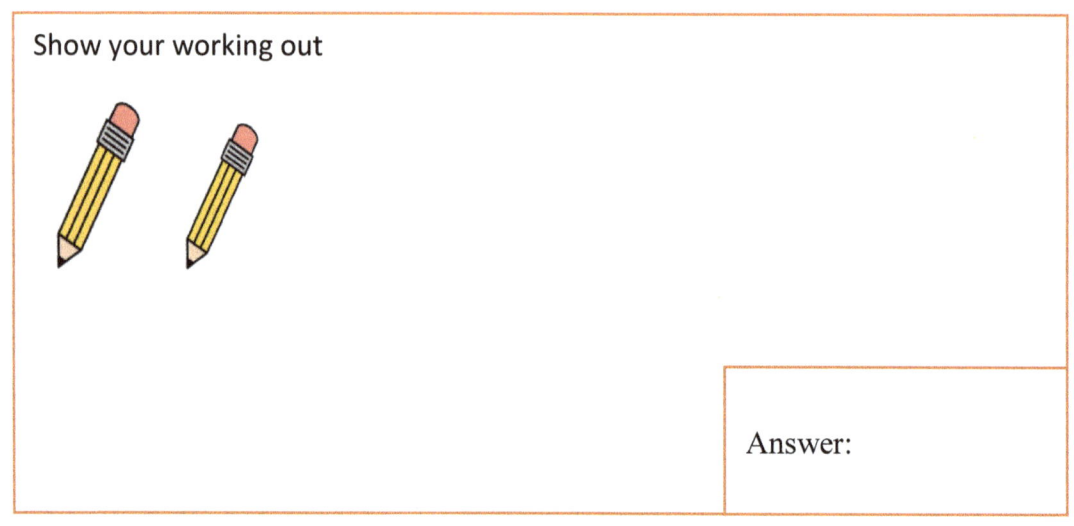

Answer:

5. You are told that 50% of the pupils in a class are boys.
What is the smallest number of pupils the class could contain?

Show your working out

Answer:

6. It takes 4 builders 10 hours to build a wall. How many hours would it have taken 5 builders to build the same wall?

Show your working out

Answer:

7. I buy 7 drinks at 72p each, and 9 sandwiches at £1.21 each.
How many change do I get from a £20 note?

Show your working out

Answer:

8. Micah bought 2 pens for £0.99 each and a pack of paper for £1.47. She gave the clerk some money and got back £1.55 in change. How much money did Micah give the clerk?

Show your working out

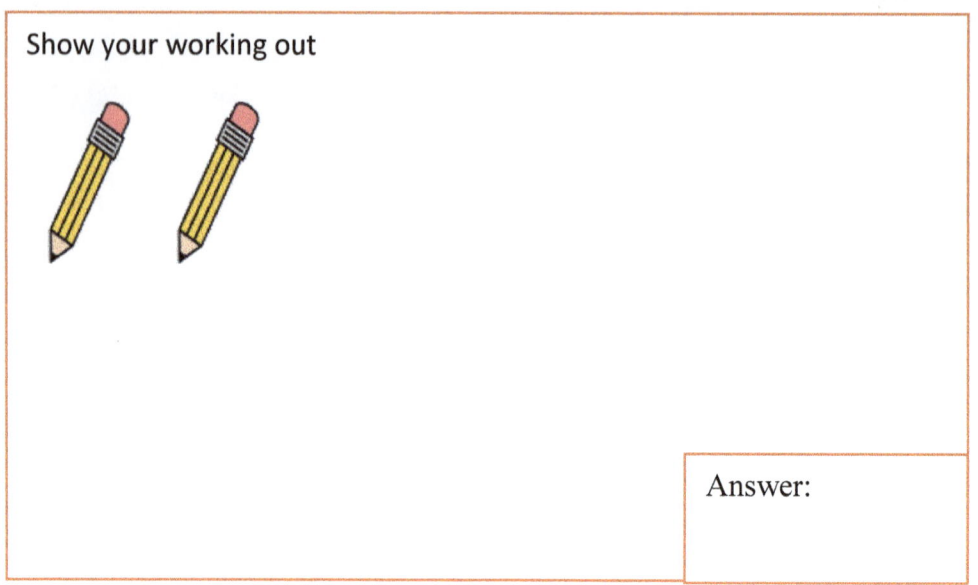

Answer:

Q9.Kent Basketball team won 80% of their games last season and had no tied games. They lost 5 games. How many games did they play altogether?

Show your working out

Answer:

10. Every 100g of brown bread contains 6g of fibre.

A small loaf of bread weights 400g and has 10 equal slices.

How much fibre is there in one slice?

Show your working out

Answer:

Score

Chapter 4

Median , mean , mode and Range

What is Mean, Median, Mode and Range?

- Mean: an average which is found by adding up all the values in a set of data and dividing it by the total number of values you added together.

- Median: the middle number in the set of values. You find it by putting the numbers in order from the smallest to largest and covering up one number on each end until you get to the middle.

- Mode: the number or value, which appears most often in the set. To find the mode, you need to count how many times each value appears.

- Range: the difference between the lowest and the highest value. To work it out, simply subtract the lowest value from the highest.

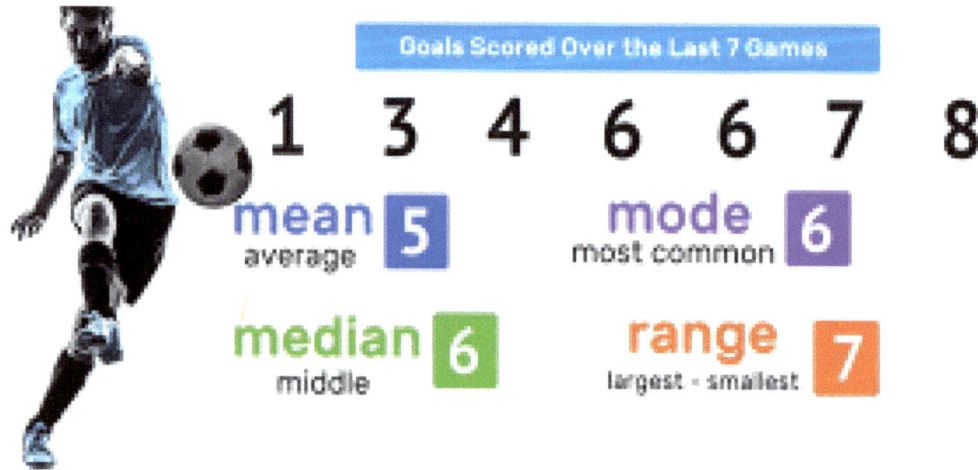

Exercise 4

Mean Median Mode Range

Hey Diddle Diddle,
the MEDIAN is the middle
You add then divide for the MEAN
- it's the average!
The MODE is the one
that appears there most
And the RANGE is
the difference between!

1. Raj made a list of his homework marks.

5, 6, 7, 8, 5, 9, 10, 4, 5, 7

    a) Write down the mode of her homework marks.

    b) Work out her median homework marks.

2. Sam rolled a 6-sided dice ten times.
Here are his scores

    3, 2, 4, 6, 3, 3, 4, 2, 5, 4

    a) Work out his median of his scores.

    b) Work out the mean of his scores.

c)Work out the range of his scores.

3.Find the mean for the following sets of data.

a)7, 11, 12, 6,4

b)14, 1, -2, -5

4.Find the median for the following set of data.

a)6, 1, 23, 14, 7

b)25, 12, 11, 16, 18, 6

5. The hotel has recorded their reviews using a frequency table.

Star rating	Frequency
0	9
1	12
2	17
3	19
4	21
5	8

For this set of data find

a)The range

b)The mode

c)The median

d)The mean

Show your working out

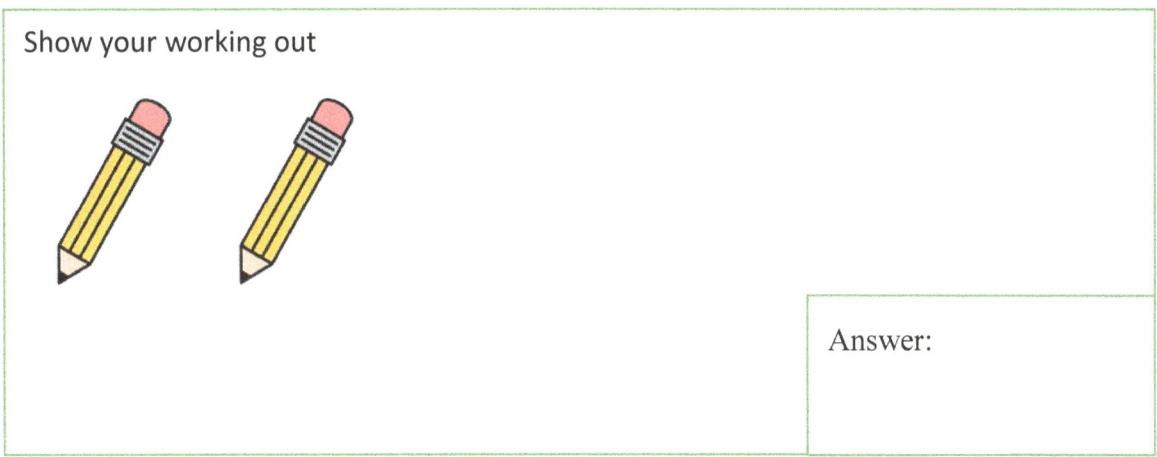

Answer:

6. Find the range of the following set of data.

a)32, 44, 33, 21, 45, 38

b)-2, -5.-2, 9, 4, 5, 11,0

7.A bar chart for the number of day ill for a group of workers is shown below .

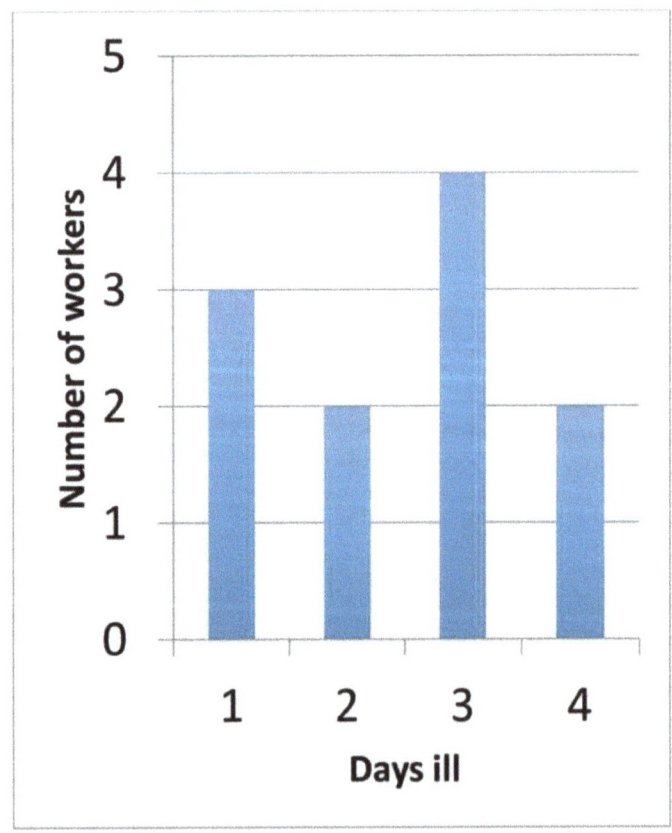

a)Find the range of the number of days ill for these workers.

b)Find the mode of the number of days ill for these workers.

c)Find the median of the numbers of days ill for these workers.

Show your working out

Answer:

The two numbers are 6.

What is the third number?

Show your working out

Answer:

9.The height of turnips are shown in the frequency table below.

Height (nearest cm)	Freq
6	3
7	8
8	12
9	4
10	1

For this set of data find
a)The range

b)The mode
c)The median
d)The mean

Show your working out

Answer:

10. The mean weight of 8 rugby players is 102kg.
The mean weight of 2 badminton players is 68kg.
Find the mean weight of all the 10 people.

Show your working out

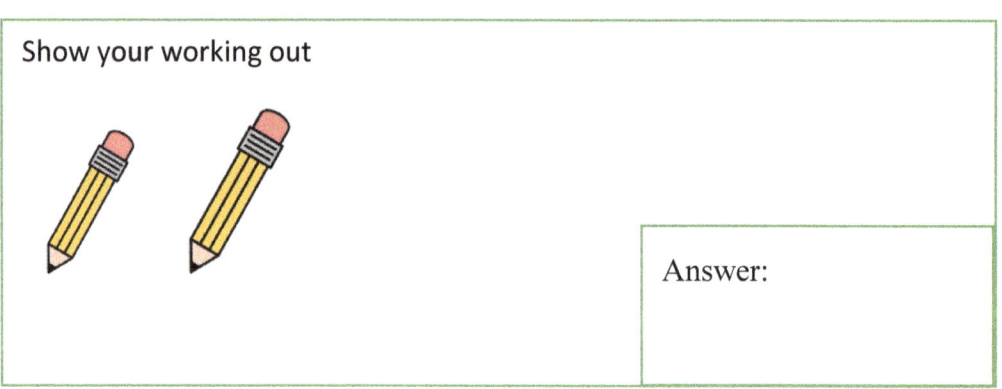

Answer:

Score

Chapter 5

Ratio and Proportion

- A ratio is a comparison of two values expressed as a quotient
  - Example: A class has 12 girls and 18 boys. The ratio of girls to boys is $\frac{12}{18}$
  - This ratio can also be expressed as an equivalent fraction $\frac{2}{3}$
- A proportion is an equation stating that two ratios are equal.
  - Example: $\frac{12}{18} = \frac{2}{3}$

A Ratio is an ordered pair of numbers 1 and 2 written as ½ where 2 does not equal 0 .

A proportion is an equation in which two ratios are set to each other.

For Example –

What is £12 as percentage £80?

$$\frac{12}{80} = \frac{percent}{100}$$

Percent = 12 x 100/80
1200/800

=15%

Another example

The sale price of a computer was £150. Which was only 80% of normal price.
What was the normal price?

$$\frac{150}{x} = \frac{80}{100}$$

= 150 x 100 /80

= 15000/80

=187.50

Exercise 5

Ratio Mixed Problems

1. There are 40 flowers in a shop, mixture of roses and tulips. If there are12 tulips, write the ratio of roses to tulips in its simplest form.

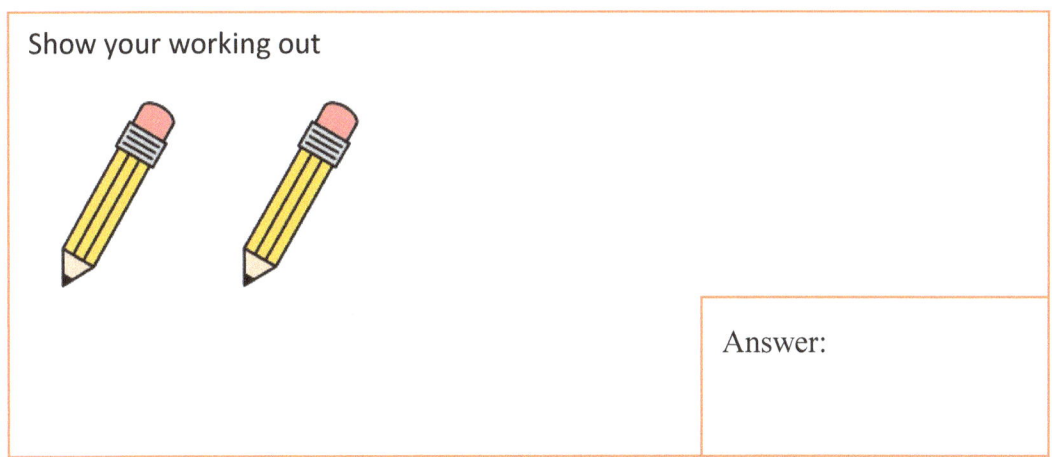

Show your working out

Answer:

2. There are bourbons and digestives in a jar. There are 36 biscuits in total. If 10 of the biscuits are bourbons, find the ratio
of bourbons to digestives in its simplest form.

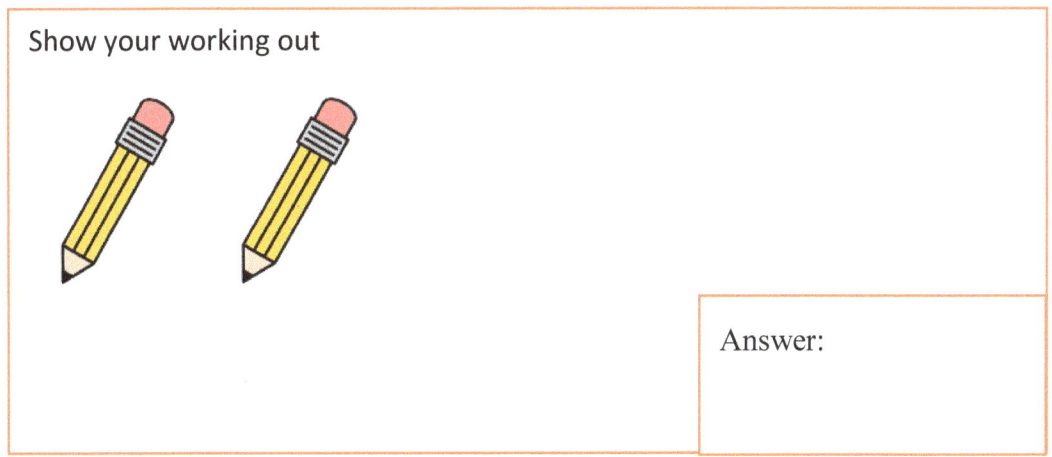

Show your working out

Answer:

3. There are 40 socks in a drawer, either
black or grey. If $\frac{3}{4}$ of the socks are black, write the ratio of black socks to grey socks
in its simplest form.

Show your working out

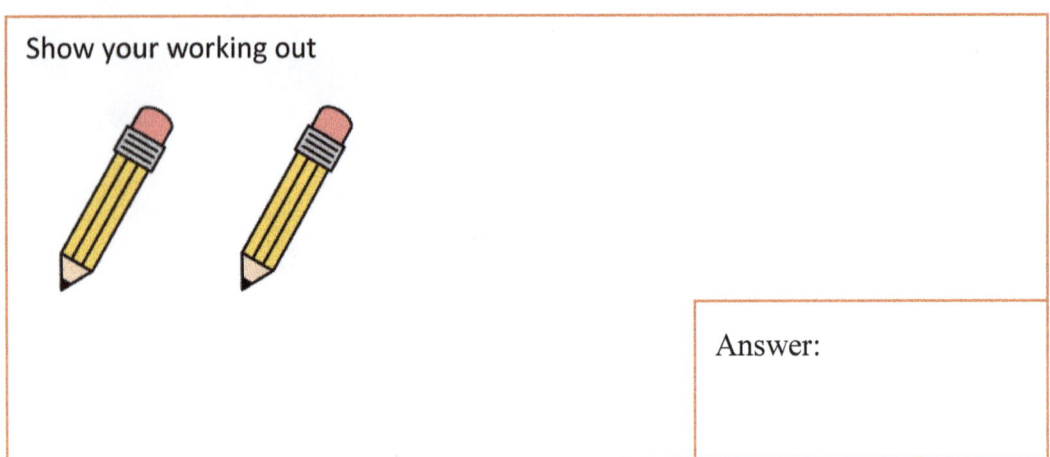

Answer:

4. The ratio of circles to squares is 6 : 1.
If there are 5 squares, how many circles are there?

Show your working out

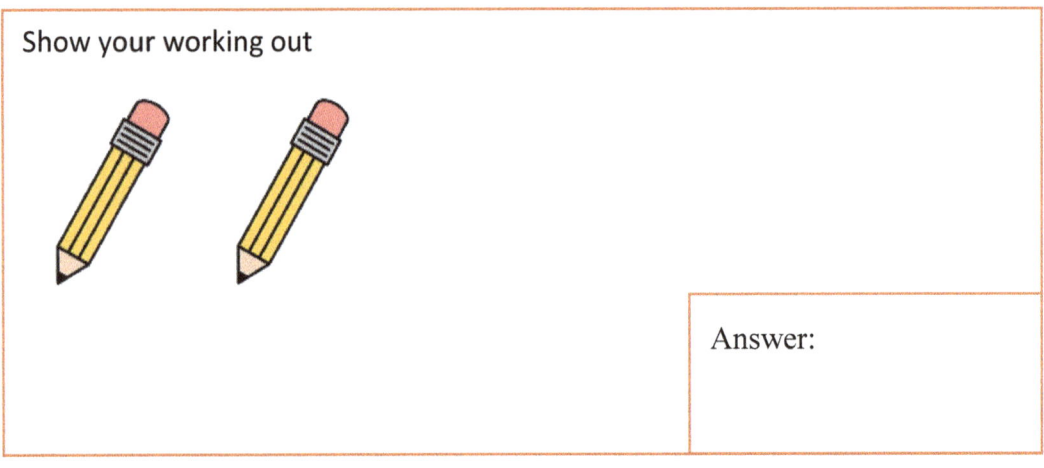

Answer:

5. At the gym, the ratio of men to
women is 7 : 3. If there are 35 men,
how many women are there?

Show your working out

Answer:

6. On a washing line there are t-shirts and jumpers in the ratio 2 : 3.
 If there are 21 jumpers, how many t-shirts are
there?

Show your working out

Answer:

7. The ratio of dogs to cats is 4 : 1. If there are 5 cats, how many animals are there in total?

Show your working out

Answer:

8.. A cafe sells cups of tea and coffee in the ratio 8 : 3. On Tuesday the café sells 72 cups of coffee.
How many cups of tea and coffee did they sell in total that day?

Show your working out

Answer:

9. Bill has a total of 50 black or white counters.
If there are 3 black counters for every 2 white counters, how many black counters are there?

Show your working out

Answer:

10. Maryam eats bananas and apples in the ratio 5 : 2. Last week she ate 8 apples.
How many bananas did she eat?

Show your working out

Answer:

11. A packet contains lime or lemon
flavour sweets in the ratio 2 : 7.
 If there are 36 sweets in total, how many are
lemon flavour?

Show your working out

Answer:

Score

Exercise 5.1 Proportion Problems

Q1. In a group of 48 children, the ratio of boys to girls is 3.5.

How many boys must join the group to make the ratio of boys to girls 5:3?

Show your working out

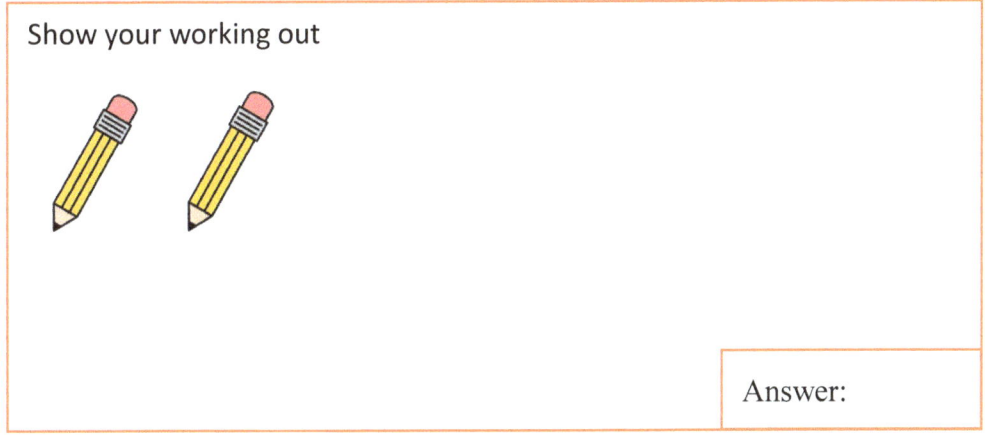

Answer:

Q2. Ram is making cookie. He mixes the flour, butter, and sugar in the ratio 6:4:1. Ram uses 160 grams of butter.
Work out how much flour and sugar Ram uses.

Show your working out

Answer:

Q3 Mary has a bag of 20 sweets.
10 of the sweets are red.
3 of the sweets are black.
The rest of the sweets are white.
Mary chooses one sweet at random.
What is the probability that Mary will choose a Red sweets

Show your working out

Answer:

Q4. A box contains trays of melons.
There are 15 melons in a try.
There are 3 trays in a box.
A supermarket sells 40 boxes of melons
How many melons does the supermarket sell?

Show your working out

Answer:

Q5. £12 is shared between Emily, Claire, and Ram in the ratio 9:5:2
How much do they receive?

Show your working out

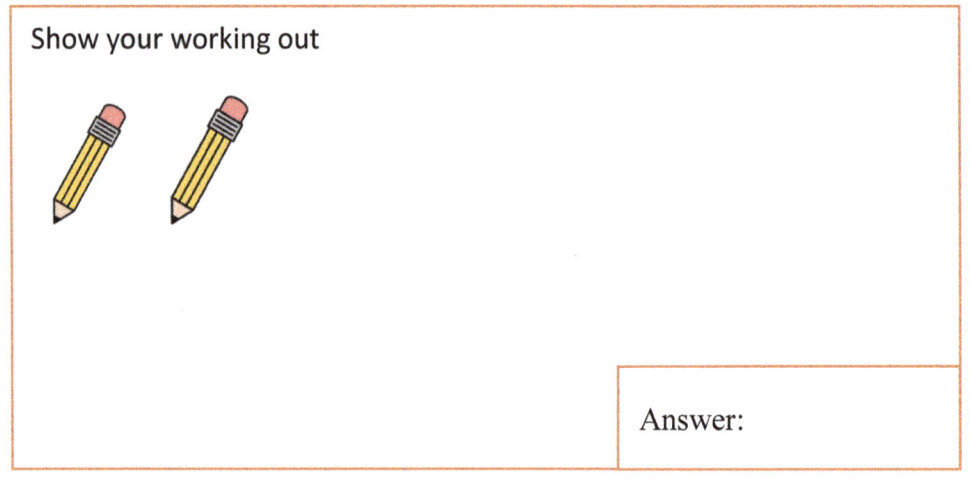

Answer:

Q6. In a school there are three times as many boys as girls. There are twice as many male teachers are female teachers. The number of boys and male teachers is 512, the number of girls and female teacher is 176.
The number of teachers is 4.
How many female teachers are in the school?

Show your working out

Answer:

Q7. There are 180 sheep in a flock. For every 9-white sheep's there is a 1 black sheep.
How many white and black sheep are there?

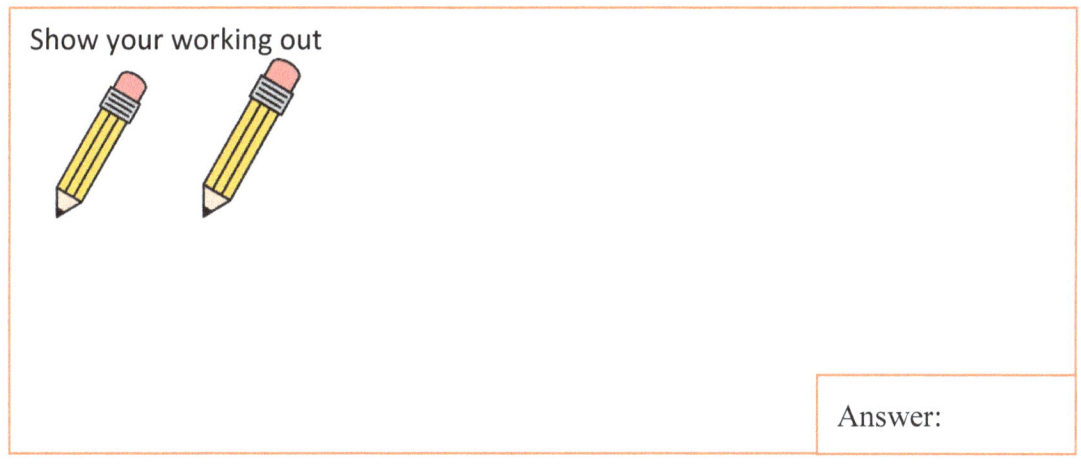

Show your working out

Answer:

Q8. There are 30 children in Class 6. 60% of them are girls
What how many girls and boys are there in the class?

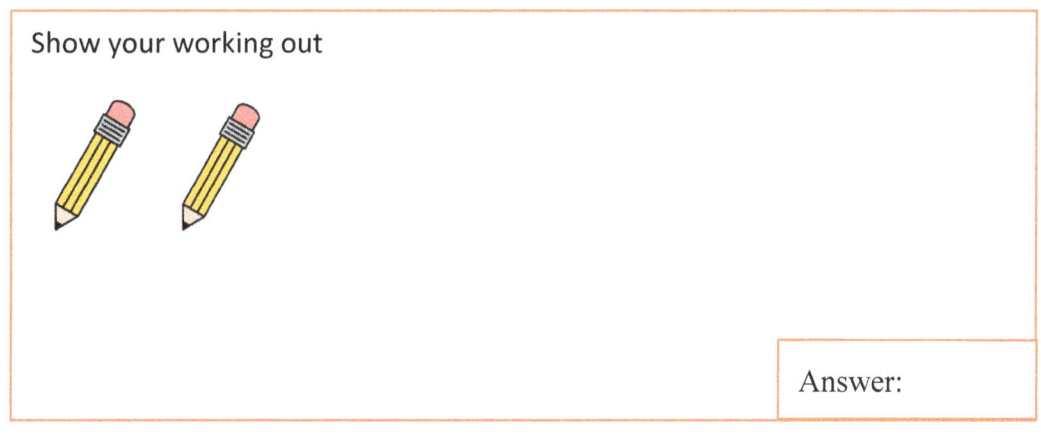

Show your working out

Answer:

Q9. The population of Delhi is 11552.
The men and children together number 8763
And the men and women number 5874.
How many women are there?
How many children are there?
How many men are there?

Show your working out

Answer:

Q10. In a class 19 children have dogs and 18 children have cats, if 15 children have both dogs and cats, find the smallest numb of children in the class.

Show your working out

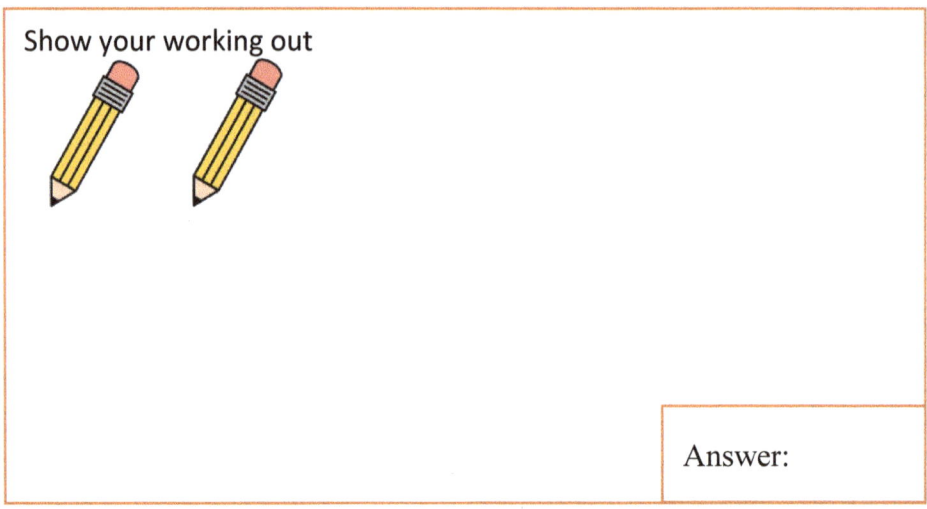

Answer:

Q11. I set a goal to drink 64 ounces of water a day.
If I drink $10\frac{1}{3}$ ounces in the morning, $15\frac{1}{2}$ ounces at noon, and $20\frac{5}{6}$ ounce at dinner, how many more ounces of water do I have to drink to reach my goal for the day?

Show your working out

Answer:

12. if $3\frac{1}{2}$ ounce of cough syrup is used from $9\frac{1}{4}$ ounce bottle, how much is left?

Show your working out

Answer:

Score

Revision Test

Q1. In February, three salesmen working in an electronic store sold a total 140 laptops. Ben sold half as many laptops as Sean, who sold half as many as Michael. Work out how many computers each of the three salesmen sold in February?

Show your working out

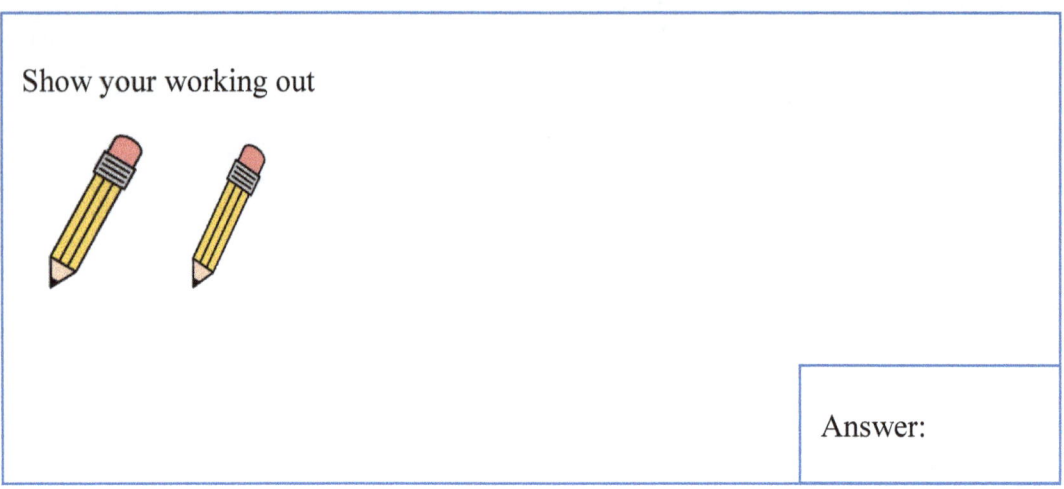

Answer:

Q2. Belinda ate $\frac{3}{5}$ of a bar of chocolate .60 grams of chocolate remained. What was the original mass of the chocolate bar?

Show your working out

Answer:

Q3. Sandy needs 12 pizzas to feed 30 people
How many pizzas will she need to feed 35 people?

Show your working out

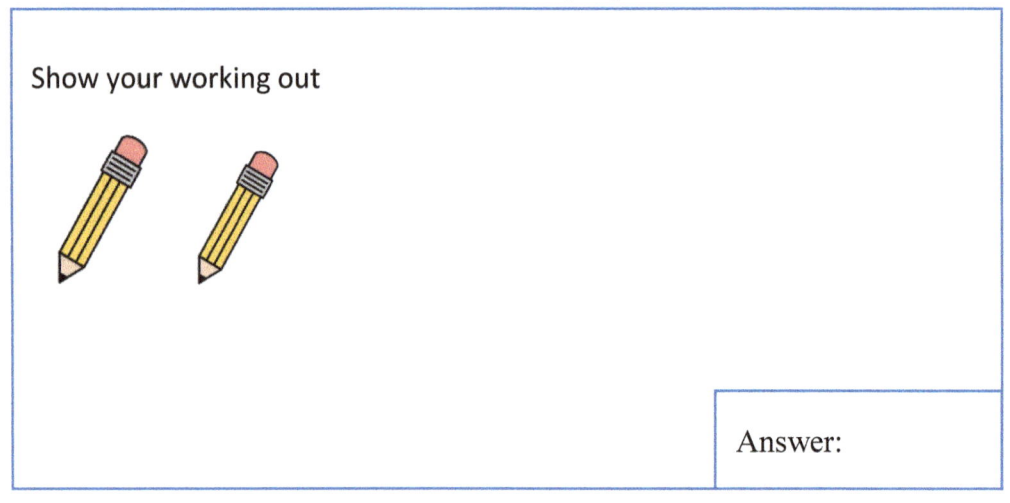

Answer:

Q4 Write down two numbers which differ by 2 and multiply to 168

Show your working out

Answer:

Q5 In a sponsored walk: Adam took 4 hours, 39 minutes;
Billy took 274 minutes and Charlie took 4 hours.
Who was quickest and who was the slowest?

Show your working out

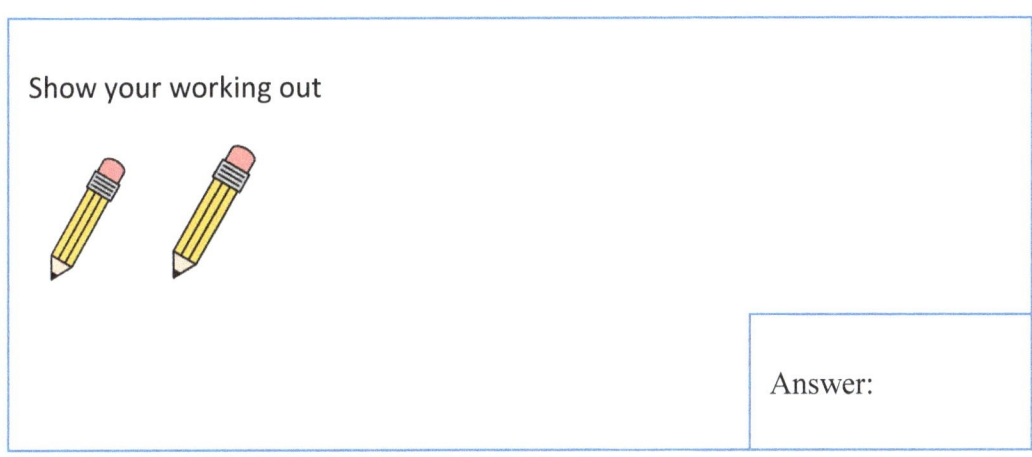

Answer:

Q6. Think of two integers that have a product of 18 and a difference that is the same as one of the two integers that you are thinking of .

Show your working out

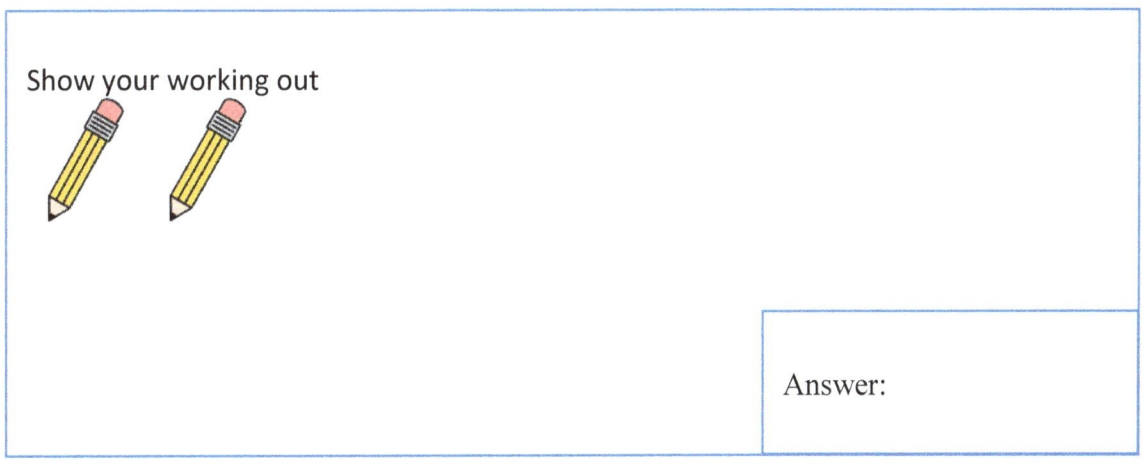

Answer:

Q7. Krishna has 1 hour to clean the house before his parents get back from their holiday. He must hoover 3 rooms, clean out his pet hamster's cage and wipe off the drawing of an elephant has accidently did on the bathroom wall. Each room takes 12 minutes to hoover, it takes 18 minutes to clean out his hamster's cage and 21 minutes to rub out the elephant, he does last.

What fraction of the elephant is left on the wall when Krishna's parents arrive home?

Show your working out

Answer:

Q8 Aldan told to divide a certain number by 17. Instead, he divided the number by 7 and got the answer 68. What was the answer to the division he was supposed to do?

Show your working out

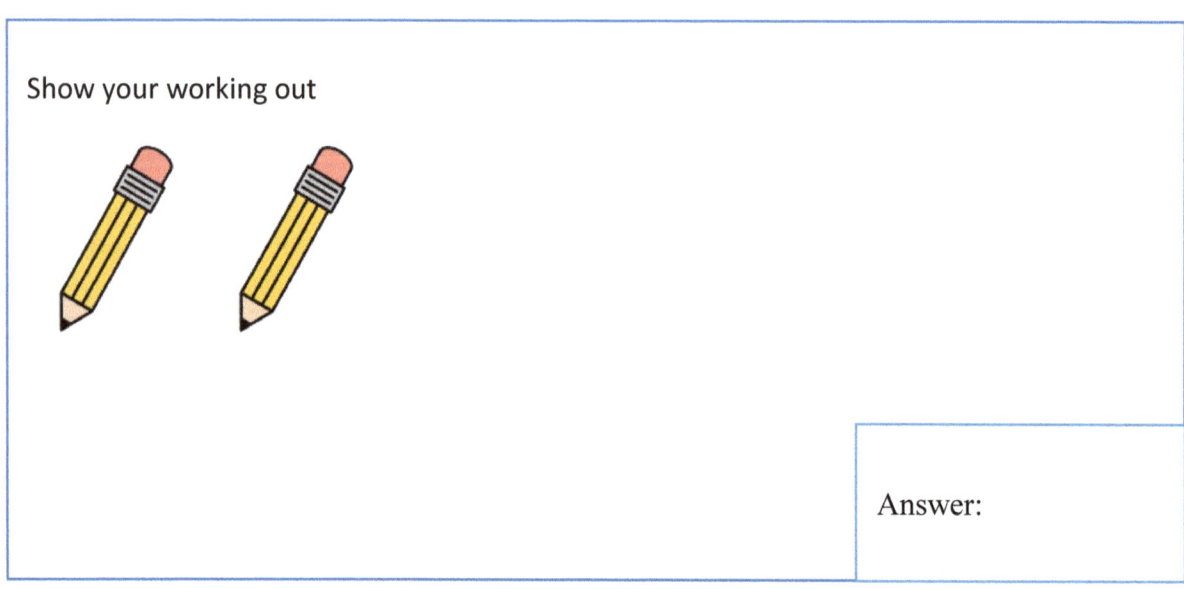

Answer:

Q9. What is the largest number less than 100 which is a multiple of 2 and of 3, and 5?

Show your working out

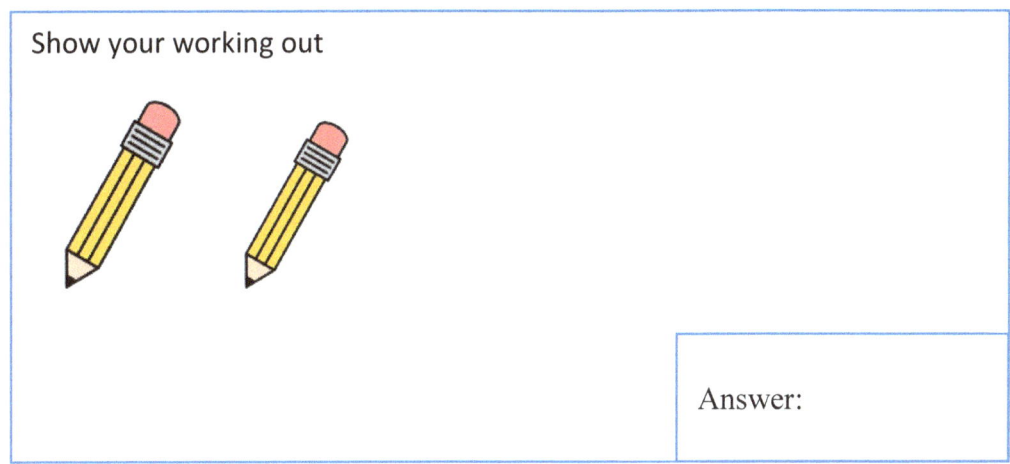

Answer:

Q10. Four bells ring at intervals of 2,8,7, and 11 seconds. if they are all rung at the same time, how many seconds will pass before they all ring at the same time again.

Show your working out

Answer:

11. At a busy railway station trains leave from platform 5 every 6 minutes and from platform 8 every 10 minutes. Trains leave from both platforms at 15:57.
when do trains next leave both platforms at the same time?

Show your working out

Answer:

Q12. How many whole numbers less than 100 cannot be divided exactly by 4 or by 5?

Show your working out

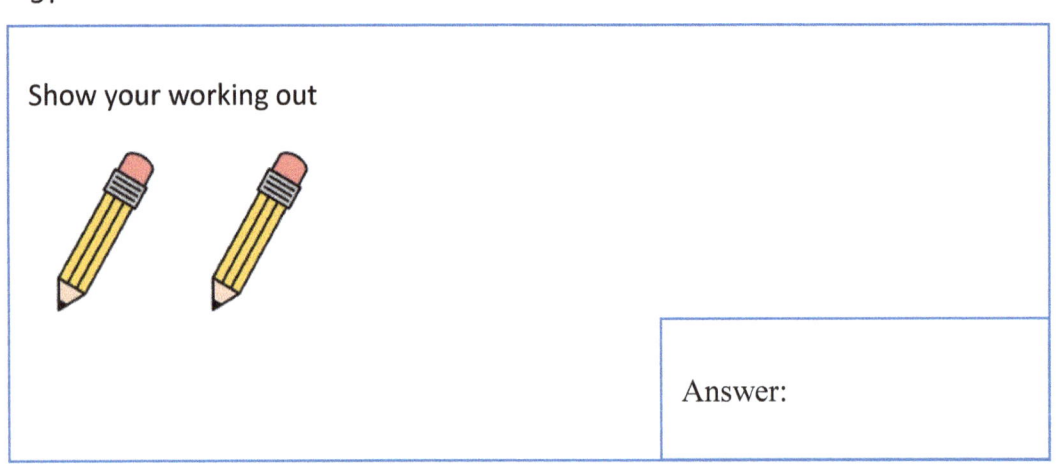

Answer:

Q13. What is the largest number that goes exactly into 90, 210 and 300?

Show your working out

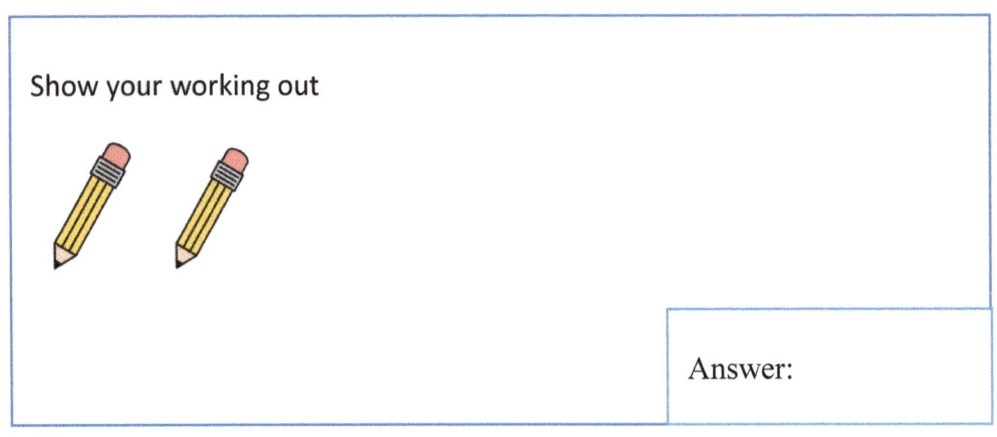

Answer:

Q14. Tim is going paintballing. Entry into paintballing costs £23,
but then also must pay   £6 per 100 paintballs than you use.
Tim spends £65 in total. How many paintballs he uses?

Show your working out

Answer:

Q15. Tyler buys 16 chicken wings and receive £14.72 change from a £20 note.
What is the price of a one chicken wings?

Show your working out

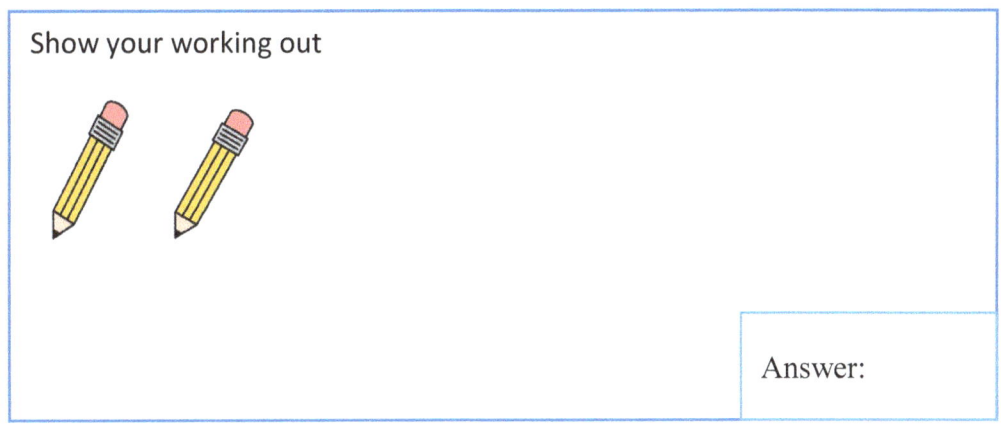

Answer:

Q16. Donald's buys three quarters of the slices in a shop.
Alisha then buys a sixth of the remaining slices.
Alisha bought 3 slices. How many more slices than Alisha did Donald's buy?

Show your working out

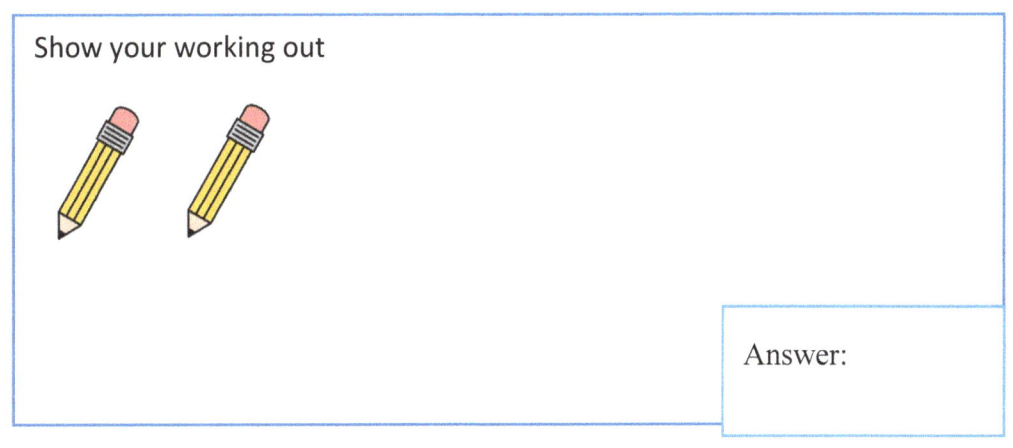

Answer:

Q17. Two shirts and three tops cost £29. Three shirts and one top cost £19. What is the cost of the top?

Show your working out

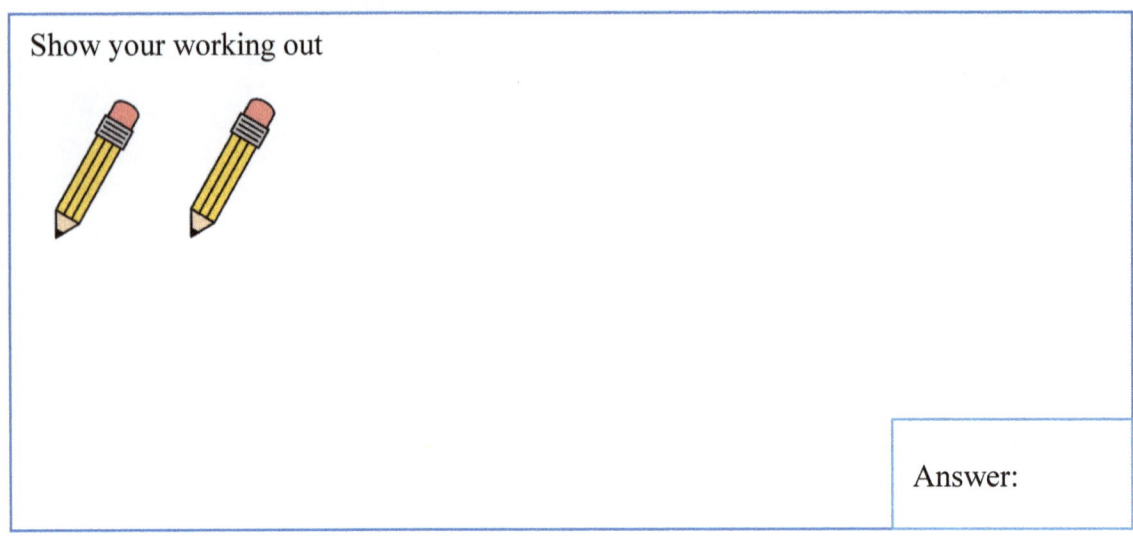

Answer:

Q18. Three CDs and DVDs cost £47. Two CDs and three DVDs cost £47. what is the cost of one CDs.

Show your working out

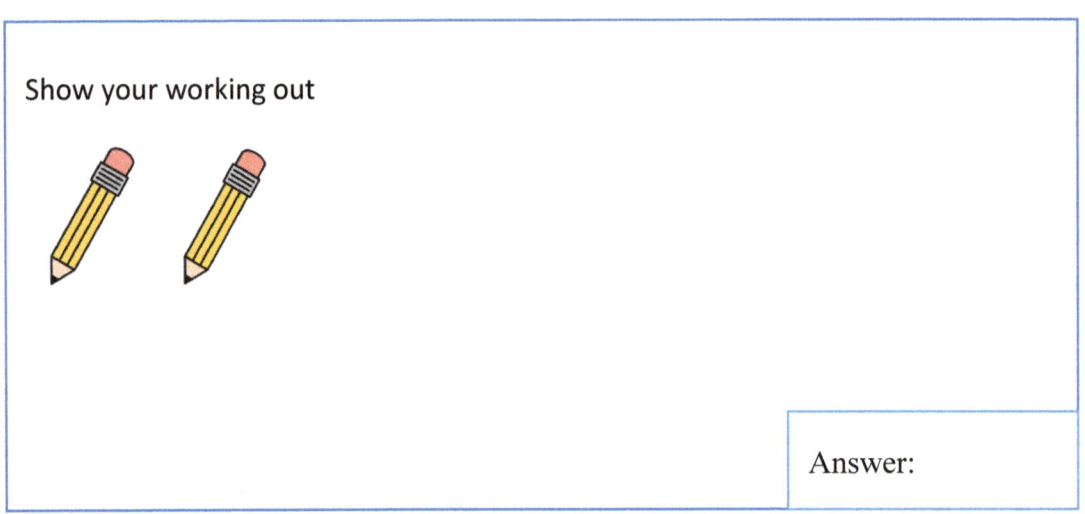

Answer:

Q19. A bull and three cows' costs of £1300. Four bulls and eight cow cost £4000.
What is the cost of the bull?

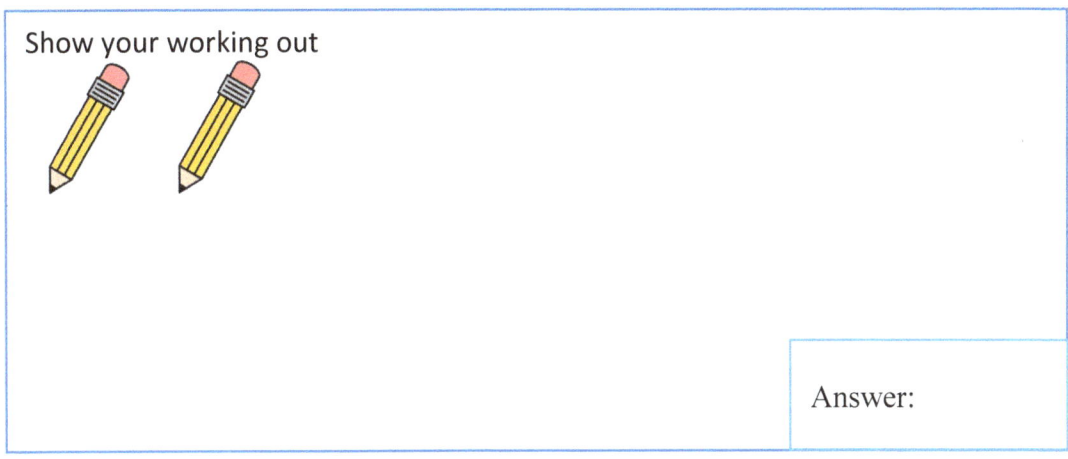

Show your working out

Answer:

Q20. Shalin has 40 helium balloons. some of the balloons are red, some are blue, and some are green. There are three times as many green balloons as there are red balloons and there are twice as many blue balloons as there are green balloons.
How many balloons are green balloons?

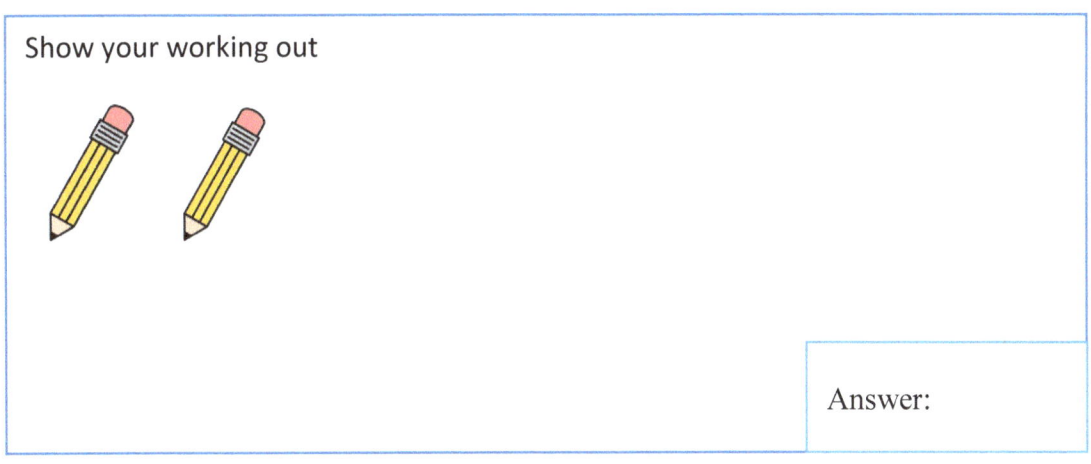

Show your working out

Answer:

Score

Answers

Exercise 1.1 (Basic)

a) ½

b) 1/6

c) 3/5

d) 3/8

e) 5/6

f) 6/12

EXERCISE 1.2 (Advance)

1) $\frac{13}{20}$

2) $\frac{2}{9}$

3) Less than ½

4) $\frac{3}{4}$

5) $\frac{5}{4}$

6) 20

7) $\frac{9}{35}$

8) 1

9) Total money spends = $\frac{5}{9}$

First time money spend is 1/3

The money spend by him is 2/3

$\frac{1}{3} \times \frac{2}{3} = \frac{2}{9}$

Altogether he spends

$\frac{1}{3} + \frac{2}{9} = \frac{5}{9}$

10) 2

11) 138

12) 48

13) $1\frac{2}{4}$

14) $\frac{32}{10}$

15) 5

16) $6\frac{1}{6}$ feet

17) $\frac{4}{3}$

18) $12\frac{1}{24}$

19) 3

20) 12

Exercise 1.3   Complete the equivalent fractions.

1. $\dfrac{2}{3} = \dfrac{12}{18}$

2. $\dfrac{9}{12} = \dfrac{81}{108}$

3. $\dfrac{18}{25} = \dfrac{90}{125}$

4. $\dfrac{3}{4} = \dfrac{18}{24}$

5. $\dfrac{1}{2} = \dfrac{7}{14}$

6. $\dfrac{4}{6} = \dfrac{36}{54}$

7. $\dfrac{2}{9} = \dfrac{8}{36}$

8. $\dfrac{2}{5} = \dfrac{6}{15}$

9. $\dfrac{1}{7} = \dfrac{2}{14}$

10. $\dfrac{1}{2} = \dfrac{4}{8}$

11. $\dfrac{3}{4} = \dfrac{30}{40}$

12. $\dfrac{6}{12} = \dfrac{36}{72}$

13. $\dfrac{1}{10} = \dfrac{8}{80}$

14. $\dfrac{1}{3} = \dfrac{5}{15}$

15. $\dfrac{2}{6} = \dfrac{12}{36}$

16. $\dfrac{7}{8} = \dfrac{42}{48}$

17. $\dfrac{3}{5} = \dfrac{24}{40}$

18. $\dfrac{12}{25} = \dfrac{24}{50}$

Exercise 1.4

1. $4 \times \frac{1}{2} =$ 2

2. $7 \times \frac{1}{4} =$ $1\frac{3}{4}$

3. $5 \times \frac{9}{10} =$ $4\frac{1}{2}$

4. $\frac{2}{3}$ of $2 =$ $1\frac{1}{3}$

5. $\frac{5}{8}$ of $1 =$ $\frac{5}{8}$

6. $\frac{1}{2}$ of $1 =$ $\frac{1}{2}$

7. $\frac{1}{6}$ of $3 =$ $\frac{1}{2}$

8. $10 \times \frac{4}{5} =$ 8

9. $\frac{1}{12}$ of $5 =$ $\frac{5}{12}$

10. $6 \times \frac{6}{12} =$ 3

11. $\frac{4}{8}$ of $3 =$ $1\frac{1}{2}$

12. $3 \times \frac{1}{10} =$ $\frac{3}{10}$

13. $\frac{2}{4}$ of $2 =$ 1

14. $\frac{1}{2}$ of $4 =$ 2

15. $9 \times \frac{4}{6} =$ 6

16. $3 \times \frac{1}{3} =$ 1

Exercise 2

1. 3:4

2. 1:4

3. 1: 3

4. 7:5

5. 2:9

6. 3:5

7. 8:9

8. 7:9

9. 8:9

10. 9:8 :6

11. 9:24:27 simplify further to 3:8:9

12. 1: 2: 4

13. 8: 9 :11

14. 6: 10: 12 simplify further to 3: 5: 6

15. 1: 4: 9

16. 6: 9: 15 simplify further to 2: 3: 5

17. 1: 2: 3

18. 30: 51 :49

19. 36: 63: 768

20. 21: 28: 24

Exercise 2.1

1. 9

2. 1.5

3. 4 to 15

4. 110

5. 27:12 simplify further to 9:4

6. 140

7. 1.8

8. Peter = £48
Sam = £32

9. Milly= 21
Zoie= 14
Ella= 7

10. 31 Boys

11. Jack= 3600
Jill = 6000

12. 10, 30, 80

13. 600

14. 2:1

15(a) 3:5

15(b) 5:8

Exercise 2.2

1. 72

2. 42

3. 188

4. 54

5.396

6.16

7.49

8.41

9. 380

10. 9

11.130

12.356

13.937

14.380

15.84

Exercise 3 (Basic) Converting Fractions, Decimals and
 Percentage

1. 22/100,22%

2.84/100,0.84

3.0.49

4.0.75,75%

5.0.98,98%

6.17/100,0.17

7. 0.92,92%

8. 0.80,80%

9. 0.27,27%

10. 44/100,0.44

11. 12/100,12%

12. 0.35,35%

13. 56/100,0.56

14. 0.99,99%

Exercise 3.1

1. 0.64%

2. 13

3. £6.75

4. 35%

5. 25 pupils

6. 8 hours

7. £4.07

8. £5

9. 25

Percentage of game won= 80%

Number of games tied= 0
Percentage of game tied= 0%
Percentage of game lost = 100% - 80% = 20%
Number of games lost = 5
20%= 5 games

10% = 2.5 games

100%= 25 games

Number of games played together= 25

10. 24 g

100g of brown bread contains 6g of fibre

4×100= 400g of brown bread contains $4 \times 6 = 24g$ of fibre

Pack of 400g contains 10 slices

Therefore, each slice contains 24/10= 2.4 g of fibre

Exercise 4

1.a) mode =5

b) median =6.5

2.a) median = 3.5
b) mean = 36/10=3.6
c) range = 4

3.a) mean =40/5=8
b) mean =8/4=2

4.a) median = 7
b) median =14
c) median = -3

5.a) The range = 5-0=5 star
b) The mode = 4 star
c) The median =3 star
d)The mean = $\dfrac{9x0+12x1+17x2+19x3+21x4 +8x5}{86.}$ =2.6 star hotel

6.a) Range =24

b) Range =13

7. a) Range =4-1 =3 days
   b)3 days
   c) Total number of workers = 11,
so halfway is the 6th number, which is 3 days

8.if the mean of 3 numbers is 7 then they must total to 21.To work out the third number, add the first two numbers and take it away from the total.
6 +6=12
21-12=9

9. a)The range is 10-4=4cm

b)The mode is 8cm

c)The median is 8cm

d)The mean = $\dfrac{3\times6+8\times7+12\times8+4\times9+1\times10}{28}$ = 216/28=7.7cm

10. The first step is to find the combined weight of all 10 people. We can do this by multiplying the mean by the number of players then adding the 2 values together:

102kg x8 = 816kg

68kg x 2 = 136kg

816kg + 136kg = 952kg

The next step is to use this to find the mean of all 10 people, we have the total weight so we just need to divide it by the number of people:

952kg ÷ 10 = 95.2kg

Exercise 5

1.Roses: tulips

   7:3

2.bourbons: fugitives

    5:13

3. Black: grey

    3:1

4.circles: square

   30: 5

5.men: women

   35 : 15

6.t-shirts: jumpers

    14: 21

7.dogs: cats

  5: 25

8.tea: coffee

72: 264

9.black counters: white counters

  30: 20 =50 counters

10. Bananas: apples
   20:8

11.lime: lemon
   28:36

Exercise 5.1

1. 32

Total number of boys and girls= 3n + 5n= 48

8n=48

N=6

Number of boys = $6 \times 3 = 18$

Number of girls= $6 \times 5 = 30$

Let's assume number of boys joining the group = x

$$\frac{x + 18}{30} = \frac{5}{3}$$

$3x + 54 = 150$
$3x = 150 - 54$

$$3x = \frac{96}{3}$$
$$x = 32$$

2. Ram uses
160/4=40
6 x 40 = 240 grams of butter and 1x40 =40 grams of sugar.

3. Probability that marry will choose a red sweet will be 10/20=1/2

4. 1800 melons

5. Emily -£6.75 , Claire = £3.75 and Ram £1.50

6. 16 female teachers

7. 162 white sheep's
18 black sheep's

8. 18 girls and 12 boys

9. There are 2789 women
There are 5678 children
There are 3085 men

10. 22

11. $17\frac{1}{3}$ ounces

12. $5\frac{3}{4}$ ounces

Revision Test 1

1.   Ben   Sean   Michael
W   2W   4W

W+2W+4W=140
7W=140
W=140/7=20
W=20

BEN =1X20=20
SEAN=2X20=40
MICHEAL=4X20=80

2. $^2/_5$ $x = 60$

$x = \frac{60}{2}$ x5= 150 g

3. Pizza per person 12/30=2/5 pizza per person

For 35 people
35 x 2/5=70/5=14
She will need 14 pizzas

4. We need two numbers that:

- differ by 2
- multiply to 168

Try factor pairs of 168: 1x 168, 2x 84, 3 x 56, 4 x42, 6 x 28, 7 x 24, ,8 x 21, 12 x 14

Only and differ by 2.

Check:

Answer: 12 and 14

5. Adam= (4×60) +
39
= 279 mins
Billy =274 mins
Charlie = (4x60) +(3/5 x60)
=240 + 36
=276 mins
Quickest is Billy and slowest is Adam

6.   3 and 6
18=1x18
=2x9
=3x6
3x6=18
6-3=3

7. 5/7

12x3 +18x1+21x 1
=36+18+21
=75 min
75-60= 15 min
15/21=5/7

8. 28

68x7=476
476/17=28

9. 90

10. 616 seconds

LCM of 2,8.7.11
=56x11
616seconds

11. 16:27

12. 59

100/5 =20, 100/4 =25

Multiples of both 4 and 5 =20,40.60.80.100/5
=100-20-25+5-1
100-41
=59

13. 30

14. 700
65-23=42
42/6=7
7x100 = 700

15. Chicken wings

Tyler pays with £20 and gets £14.72 change.

So he actually spent:

£20-£14.72 =£5.28
He bought 15 chicken wings so the price for each chicken wings
5.28/16=0.33

16. 51 more slices of turkey than Alisha

1/24 x=3(Alisha)
X=3x24=72(total)

3/4x72=54(Donald's)
    54-3=51

17. £7
2x+3y=29
3x+y=19
9x+3y=57
7x=57-29
X=28/7=4
2(4) +3y=8+3y=29
=3y=21
Y=21/3=7

18. C = cost of one CD

    D = cost of one DVD

3C+4D=47

2C+3D=47

Eliminate D

Multiply the first equation by **3**:

9C+ 3D=141

Subtract the second equation

(9C+ 3D) − (2C+ 3D) =141-47

7C=94/7=13.48

C=13.43

19.£400

20.

- R = red balloons
- G = green balloons
- B = blue balloons

We are told:

- Total balloons = 40
- Green are 3 times red:
- Blue are twice green:

    Green are 3 times red:G=3R

    Blue are twice green:B=2G

    R+G+B=140

    Substitute G=3R and B =2G=6 R

    R+ 3R+6R=40

    10R=40

    R=40/10

    R=4

    Find Green balloons

    G=3R=3(4) =12

www.ingramcontent.com/pod-product-compliance
Lightning Source LLC
Chambersburg PA
CBHW041947010726
47475CB00042BA/522